Luminance

Luminance

Thomas Fasano

Coyote Canyon Press

Copyright © 2025 by Thomas Fasano

All rights reserved.

No part of this publication may be reproduced, distributed, or transmitted in any form or by any means, including photocopying, recording, or other electronic or mechanical methods, without the prior written permission of the author, except in the case of brief quotations embodied in critical reviews and certain other noncommercial uses permitted by copyright law.

First Edition

Table of Contents

Entanglement 1
Ebbing Pulse 2
Urban Pirouette 3
Tendrils 4
Entangled Resonance 5
Honeycomb Geometry 6
Heliotropic Arithmetic 7
Entwined Exchanges 8
Urban Echoes 9
Lichen's Tapestry 10
Fractal Currents 11
Molecular Sanctuary 12
Erosion's Hymn 13
Ephemeral Threads 14
Webwork 15
Effervescence 16
Abyssal Illuminations 17
Inertia 18
Photon Whispers 19
Entropy's Reverie 20
Cosmic Pulse 21
Erosion's Embrace 22
Photonarratives 23
Transience 24
Glacial Whispers 25
Resonant Weave 26
Luminescence 27
Symbiosis 28
Glacial Imprint 29
Chronicles of Rings 30

Bioluminescent Echoes	31
Erosion's Reverie	32
Fibonacci's Whisper	33
Unraveling	34
Ephemeral Geometry	35
Potentiality	36
Bioluminescent Reverie	37
Fleeting Geometry	38
Symphony of Currents	39
Luminance	40
Lattice of Light	41
Cradle Currents	42
Twilight Lattice	43
Photonics	44
Ephemeral Whirl	45
Catalytic Whispers	46
Refraction	47
Erosion's Echo	48
Tidal Wisdom	49
Mycelial Exchange	50
Ephemeral Flux	51
Pulse of Permeation	52
Celestial Drift	53
Stellar Alchemy	54
Molecule Dance	55
Twisted Histories	56
Spectral Currents	57
Stitchery	58
Helix	59
Vital Currents	60

Entangled Currents	61
Hexagonal Symphony	62
Neon Cartography	63
Ebbing Constellations	64
Erosion	65
Unfolding	66
Porecraft	67
Ethereal Flux	68
Prismatic Whispers	69
Entangled Grace	70
Stardust Whispers	71
Thawing Choreography	72
Cosmic Threads	73

Entanglement

a particle waltzes:
a quark, a dance
in the weightless expanse of
    where resonance thrums in
the fabric,
each change ripples—an echo
    a cosmos entwines:
thoughts like photons,
  interpenetrate like threads in
the universe swells,
inhales, exhales,
consciousness brims in the
quantum sea

Ebbing Pulse

the dawn unfurls: light spills:
a liquid prism over the
surface of the sea: hues converse—
pearl and slate, the horizon's
growing breath imbues the chill—
each wave a whisper: reflecting
the mind's own rippling thoughts:
a blue shimmer stirs, then recedes,
echoing the tides, an ebbing pulse—
the heart knows:
change is constant.

Urban Pirouette

the city dawns:
starlings pirouette
through hazy skies, where
LED constellations flicker:
they misread dawn,
navigating glow with the grace
of instinct
traffic hums beneath:
the pulse of breast and bone,
wings flexing in a language
of urban adaptation,
the commute becomes a ballet,
pavement shimmering with potential
neon heavens disrupt the dark:
are they lost, or merely
rewriting maps of migration—
each chirp a counterpoint,
each flurry a response
to the rhythm of a city waking?
among the concrete, they find
nests in eaves and ledges,
familiarity, an emergent pattern:
dimensionality compresses
the spiraled routes of flight,
    as nature threads through wires
and walls.

Tendrils

moss collects in quiet clusters:
green constellations thread through
the bark's rough maps of time: each
minute, a slow unfolding:
the growth
is mathematical: forms spiral,
intersecting like paths of light,
   when shadows stretch,
life finds a way:
tendrils whisper secrets to air,
communicating with the silence:

Entangled Resonance

across the room: a shimmer of air
bristles with whispers: secrets in
the weave of our breathing:
each pulse,
a particle colliding: entangled
    thoughts resonate through
walls: waves
traveling in quantum
motions, bending
between the distances: hearts in
silence collide:
a glance refracts light
into a spectrum: laughter threads
through ether—bonds made of
invisible strings: we listen to
    the hum of shared
resonance, merging

Honeycomb Geometry

constructed in hexagons:
the bees weave their worlds—
syrup-sweet chambers filled
with the dim hum of industry:
where light refracts through wax:
each cell a calculus of void,
a geometry of labor:
we learn from their unity—
the dance of pollen in sunlight:
individuals forming the whole:
navigating through air's embrace,
their rhythm a lesson in flow:
within the walls of this hive:
the interstice sings of purpose—
blood of the earth flows through:
order emerging from chaos—

Heliotropic Arithmetic

in the garden:
the sun's gold spirals,
each seed a small universe
arranged in Fibonacci: curves
of purpose, nature's arithmetic,
the spiral dances: a heliotropic
embrace of sunlight's gentle grip,
each turn a choice, a way to
maximize and optimize, life's
growth unfurling:
each petal, an echo
of mathematics, the beauty of order
in chaos, a florist's geometry,
where random appears, but isn't,
the wind whispers: in the rustle of
leaves, a conversation of atoms,
each seed a chapter, waiting,
in a narrative written by light.

Entwined Exchanges

beneath the surface: the dark humus
where bacteria mingle:
unseen, they twirl,
fissioning and merging in the damp,
an endless cycle of life: decay's
preparation for rebirth:
all entwined
dead leaves whisper:
nutrients weave—
carbon compounds slipping
through time,
fungal networks stretch:
highways of fate,
mycelia inhale: exhale the breath
   of earth—tiny architects of
the dance proceeds:
each microbe's task,
metabolism shifts: a potent rhythm,
    nitrogen exchanged in
delicate hands,
every decay a portal to growth:
the grand exchange of energy flows
in this circular realm:
I ponder life,
   how death teaches life:
a lesson written
in the language of roots
and spores,
the interconnectedness: we yield,
in this odyssey of being, we grow.

Urban Echoes

pigeons perch between the concrete:
their wings, a fluttering echo of
    the city's shifting pulse—breath
while by broad balconies, they sift
through crumbs of
yesterday's meals:
the architects of adaptation thrive
soft coos resonate in alleyways:
plastic glimmers, littered remnants
of human haste; they gather light—
each flapping wing,
a small revolution:
in the urban garden, they are
the shadows of
existence, reclaiming sky

Lichen's Tapestry

lichen enters: a gentle fur,
cyanobacteria and fungi bind:
to the granite's harsh countenance,
decay beckons, while life unfolds,
each layer a whisper of
time's hand.
the rock breathes: a slow sigh,
cracks filled with green and gray:
  moisture clings in the
cool crevices,
where sunlight spills:
a golden thread,
    stitching together
resilience's cloth.
as seasons turn: the colors shift,
    invisible arguments of soil
and stone,
photosynthesis weaving light:
the unhurried conversation of life—
   from death,
a tapestry of beginnings.

Fractal Currents

the diatom's silicate fronds:
perched on the brink of water,
that gleam like mathematical dreams
etched by light, refracting thought
among the currents, they spiral,
singular cells in a vast ballet:
rivers of nutrient and
light converge,
a dance of
photosynthesis, unfolding
each minute creature, a universe,
tethered by the thread of life,
radiating oxygen into air,
while tides whisper their
eternal changes
    as the microbe's beauty shapes
    and the web of life
grows intricate—
    in the smallest lens lies
a history,
each fractal echoing cosmic design

Molecular Sanctuary

    the window breathes:
its misted surface
maps a universe of droplets: worlds
in kinetic flux, merging, falling,
like thoughts coalescing in
the chill outside whispers:
gas and liquid,
    a dance of molecules,
spinning, colliding,
as light refracts through
the water's edge:
I sit in this warmth: a sanctuary,
the storm creates a canvas

Erosion's Hymn

the frost creeps in: a shiver
splits the granite's ancient face,
filling each fissure with whispered
ice, that relentless tempo of
change cascading down, down, down
a symphony of silence surrounds:
each grain released dances,
becoming part of the mountain's
slow erosion, a hymn of release,
time's slow hand molding
stone, flesh
when the wind carries fragments:
they ride the currents—dust to sky,
remnants of solidity shifting
to whispering possibilities,
the mountain's tale told
in particles
the sunlight fractures through—
a spectrum of moments, refracted,
lending warmth to the cold,
as life clings in tenacity,
the cycle of giving, receiving
and amidst this slow surrender:
the cosmos vibrates, and so
the earth's pulse resonates—
in the dance of the elements,
we, too, yield to the constant flow

Ephemeral Threads

the late sun fingers against the
cracked pavement: shadows elongate,
stretching like
aspirations, diffusing
    into shapes that pulse with
the heartbeat
of wind: particles dance
through the light
bending perception in this
brief hour
each blade of grass knows
its place—
rooted in the telling earth,
of the shadow's swift passage:
dialogue between future and fading,
as the sun threads gold through
  weaving moment with
memory, ephemeral
insects hum around the languid
warmth: their wings a
flickering pause,
reminders of the time's soft drift:
what do we chase if not the shadows
of our own becoming, the flicker of
presence against absence,
a dance of light?

Webwork

silken threads spin in light
the spider, architect of her fate—
each filament a choice, a decision
made in molecular dance, weaving
   the air with whispers of
tensile strength,
a triumph of evolution's blueprint:
how she calculates the vectors—
a web poised against the
unquiet world,
with ambush fused to artistry—
   draped between branches,
its architecture
informs the curious and the hungry:
the balance of life hangs on
her craft:

Effervescence

the powder rests:
a quiet white pile
awaiting a partner: the vinegar,
tangy, alive, a promise of fizz—
chemical chaos erupts:
bubbles rise,
the dance of molecules in
transient play
each effervescent sphere of carbon
    dioxide floats:
a moment's exhalation,
the kitchen alight
with metamorphosis,
   life's essence mirrored
in reaction—
transforming simplicity
into riotous joy

Abyssal Illuminations

the ocean's dark embrace:
light pulses, rhythmic and soft:
creatures of the abyss,
not mere shadows or wisps,
but conduits of a deep pulse,
illuminating the unseen void
in the depths: a symphony of
chemiluminescence—
squid and jellyfish weave
stories through the dark:
the pattern of existence
resounds in the murmurs,
cells aglow in the quiet,
clinging to darkness like
a theory of life waiting,
its equations unwritten,
a blueprint scattered like
starlight across vast waters
to ponder this glow:
what lies between each pulse?
isn't every flicker a life,
tangled in currents unseen,
searching: for meaning,
unraveling the cosmic quilt?

Inertia

the trees stand like sentinels:
bark thickening under frost's
unforgiving touch, colors shift:
from vibrant browns to muted
grays—a weave of time, stillness
each crack a whisper: the wind
conveys stories carried through
splintered layers, age rings swell,
like thoughts deepening in silence,
the earth exhales a breath of cold
the sap pauses, a moment of
inertia: the cycle, an arrow
looping back, resilient roots
hold tight beneath the brittle,
resist as seasons insist on change

Photon Whispers

light dances through the vacuum:
each photon a whisper of the void,
with wave-like ripples undulating,
truth bending at the edges
of thought
as particles collide
with perception:
their duality fraught with mystery
yet clear as a breeze over water,
a prism refracting hidden spectra
   we wander amid this
sprawling cosmos:
where every glimmer holds
a question,
   each flicker a chance
for connection,
the universe sighs,
expanding, breathing
  in this vastness,
time loops and folds:
infinite moments coalesce
and drift,
our minds grasping at the beyond,
   while shadows of certainty
flicker, wane

Entropy's Reverie

beneath layers of soil,
dark and damp:
a plastic bottle waits, whispers
of a time when it held
liquid light:
the sun, in rising arcs,
dapples leaves that fold and break—
the leaves dissolve,
quick as thought,
into whispers of carbon, slipping
through roots seeking sustenance:
the earth's warm embrace:
    its secrets shared in the
slow dance—
  yet here lies the
bottle, unyielding,
  inviting microbes,
the unseen throng,
to feast—yet they
turn, disinterested,
    wrapped in the thick air of
the forest:
    is it not strange how
life withers?—
a tension pulses between
life's fragility
and the stubbornness of
what remains:
the plastic holds no memory,
caged in time,
while the leaves spiral,

breath after breath,
into a new existence—

Cosmic Pulse

in the vast dark: the click,
the pulse: a cosmic rhythm—a
plunge into the heart-like glow,
pulsars spinning, momentarily
echoing the structure of time,
a meter of endless becoming—
they hurl light into the void—
each wave a memory, a thought,
spanning light-years to reach us,
the silence between beats:
a vastness swelling, contracting,
narratives lost yet felt in
the bones—
the sky unfolds: a canvas—
where particles dance like dust,
and the ethereal warmth of
gravity caresses, holds, releases,
a non-linear progression,
    the universe sighs, expands,
then waits—

Erosion's Embrace

the mountain stands:
a titan enshrined
in sediment and stone,
whispers of eons
etched deep in the
strata—fossils loom
time drips like water,
a glacier's soft sigh
carving the contours of
existence, while
the winds carry stories,
summoning them forth
as rocks crumble,
softening edges, we find
within the bones of the ancients:
that cradles our
own—roots entwined, alive

Photonarratives

the light of quasars pierces
distant beacons pulsing through
each photon a messenger from depths
   beyond our grasp,
illuminating dust.
     like clumps of thought in
the brain:
those clouds of cosmic matter,
intersecting with radiant
trails that shift,
we weave narratives out of silence.
   here we stand,
observers of the vast,
our minds like
telescopes, converging
as the universe breathes in
   the dance of light and
shadow unfolds.

Transience

the kettle hums softly: water
bubbling, the heat: a dance of
molecules stirring, chaotic, free—
steam rises, wispy forms bending,
a vaporous handshake with the air:
loss and gain entwined in
the light—
energy transfers, each drop of heat
slips from the vessel, a soft sigh,
echoes of transformation: the past—
the fleeting flicker of moments,
like steam through
fingers: fleeting,
the essence of change:
life unfolds—

Glacial Whispers

the glacier's sigh: a slow retreat
etches the earth with quiet hands—
ancient sediments whisper:
once, this was deep, dark water;
now, the stones awaken, wait.
crevasses reveal twisted roots—
decay and rebirth entwined:
the crumbling rock, a cradle,
in its powdered form: black, gray,
waiting for the kiss of life.
time swirls as cycles bend:
moss carpets the forgotten stone,
each leaf a meteorological map,
and life, like light, dances—
patterns unfolding, making whole.

Resonant Weave

the tuning fork resonates:
a sharp silver tone
ripples through air molecules,
disturbing the stillness
waves, like shadows, stretch
into corners where light holds,
intertwined with the pulse
of a tree swaying gently
echoes speak in whispers,
scientific symphony of
pressure and frequency:
the spectrum of connection
each vibration a thread
in the fabric of being
weaving invisible paths
between us: a chorus, alive

Luminescence

the night pulls back its
curtain: waves
of dark liquid hold their secrets:
bioluminescent blooms pulse softly
underneath—the plankton
weave light,
oxygen's own hymn, a thousand stars
caught in a single drop of ocean:
a dance of energy from sun to tide,
transfers of photons,
each flicker a
reminder that life flows and ebbs,
the fragile thread of
existence knots
in the dark,
each gram of salt brine,
the songs of decay ride
the currents,
  as nutrients swirl in
cycles unbroken,
and every flickering
spark proclaims
the interwoven fate of sea and sky

Symbiosis

in the cool underbellies of green
the ants move with purpose:
delicate, they lift the weight of
the world on sinewy backs—
a silent commerce of nectar
    flows from aphids,
they siphon sweet life
on the undersides of soft leaves,
the aphids cluster: small, soft
bodies pulsing with survival,
sacrificing few for many—
steeped in the warmth of sun,
each exchange a whisper of trust
a balance: a delicate equation
where one thrives only in
the other's
silent agreement to stay close—
to share warmth in the shadowed
thicket of blades and stems,
the language of touch speaks
louder than sound
and thus: the cycle spins,
nectar for safety, workers and
nurturers entwined in earth's
steady pulse, life pulled into
the rhythm of laboring hearts—
    adrift yet anchored in the
soil's embrace

Glacial Imprint

the glacier moves: slow as thought
the weight of eons presses down
carving valleys, unearthing layers:
ancient sediment, memories freeze
    intermingled with whispers
of fossils:
each crystal of ice,
a time capsule—
beyond the granite,
a history breathes
the rocks hold stories:
tectonic shifts
in silence,
they witness change's dance:
the crevices fill with green,
a dialogue of decay and rebirth
the earth's patience:
sculptor of time—

Chronicles of Rings

    the tree's rings speak:
a quiet whisper
etched into wood:
drought years narrow,
survival's fierce grip:
expansion expands
like lungs in the spring,
breathing in
    moisture, light:
the dance of cells turning,
horizons of time:
the sap's slow ascent,
tiny rivers winding through
of bark and heartwood:
the past distilled
  in concentric circles,
witness to storms,
   and sunlit days,
a testament of hope.

Bioluminescent Echoes

in the dark tide pools, almost
subliminal: tiny lives pulse,
plankton swirl, glowing like
unwritten thoughts: soft flickers
of bioluminescence in the womb
of night—where the ocean folds
its mysteries into foam: an
invisible dance: each flicker
a passage of light, a current
of energy flowing: connecting
micro to macro—atoms breathe,
collide, grow: the shoreline, a
canvas where small truths paint
the vastness of shadows—two worlds:
what fragility holds this balance?
each wave that crashes seems to
whisper—evolution's script,
the endless cycle: each organism,
an echo: "here I am, I am here,"
interwoven: life writes its tale

Erosion's Reverie

the limestone gives way:
each drop of water carries
the weight of eons—
the fossilized whispers of waves
within the cave's breath:
history folded like salt,
quarried and pressed between
layers of soft sediment,
each drip like a heartbeat,
revealing soft curves of shells,
every mariner's tale pressed
into the chalky walls—flukes
an echo of past tides:
they ebb, they flow, they settle—
in their quiet drift, life
exhumes stories lost to dark.

Fibonacci's Whisper

the spiral of seeds: a mathematic
dance unfurling in golden light:
each seed a point in space:
of growth—nested,
yet yearning for air—
the Fibonacci whispers:
count, trace
the curve of becoming, a symmetry.
the wind carries dreams:
each gust lifts
  the soft petals:
they quiver, unfold,
echoing arrangements of numbers—
joining and mingling, they sway in
  the rhythm of sunlight:
an algorithm
of beauty,
the logic of nature's hand.

Unraveling

beneath the surface: cells pulsate
in quiet, relentless
motion: enzymes
    gnaw at the edifice of fur
it's a slow, deliberate unraveling:
the cycle blooms—molecules unspooling
the mottled earth, a canvas for
the unseen artisans: bacteria teem
in wild, chaotic pirouettes: life
turns to feast,
dissolving rigid forms
into the soft mists
of nutrient-rich soil
  the air thickens:
rich with histories,
the scent of decay woven into
the fabric of the ecosystem:
each pulse a testament to harmony—
consumption begets
creation: nothing dies
yet in this quiet concert of loss,
    the winds carry whispers of
a dance of atoms,
the imprints linger
  on the skin of the
world: transient,
yet connected in the
endless refrain

Ephemeral Geometry

    the snowflakes fall:
a delicate weave
of crystalline artistry:
six-sided prisms
twisting in the air: each unique,
a fractal map of weathered breath,
their contours whisper to the wind,
as if to say: this too shall change
underneath the lens:
geometry unfolds,
hydrogen bonds: a ballet of forces,
the quicksilver dance of entropy:
a moment frozen, yet on the cusp,
melting into rivulets: life's brief
    stream: carrying whispers
of winter's end

Potentiality

a battery sits in a
darkened drawer:
    its zinc core whispers
of potential,
the copper-plated past waits for
the cathode, an unassuming relic:
once vibrant, now shadowed by dust;
the terminals dream of
connection, of flow
in a world of charged particles:
electrons poised like thoughts
they linger in silence,
ready to leap

Bioluminescent Reverie

the ship's passage stirs the
rippling currents of
blue-green glows
bioluminescent whispers rise:
a fleeting trace of life's fervor,
   the water awakens,
pulsating vibrancy
  each tiny organism,
a spark of motion,
a dance for survival:
collective choreography,
humans above,
ignorant of the glow beneath
as the wake fades,
brief luminosity,
the vastness swallows light,
a depth of connection:
ancient rhythms pulse,
time dissolving into the
night's embrace

Fleeting Geometry

frost flowers lace the windowpane:
delicate crystals bloom in silence,
   each a fleeting star,
born of breath,
their symmetrical elegance holds
the whisper of warmth just
outside this chill:
temperature dips, molecules shiver—
   water vapor,
a dance of light and darkness,
transforms, crystallizing moments
into intricate patterns
that shimmer
with the breath of dawn's
hesitant touch:
   what makes beauty linger,
then vanish,
a physics of presence, a soft thaw?
the ephemeral glistens, reflects
the world beyond, moments entwined
   in the fragile geometry
of existence:
as sunlight refracts, amplifying
the sharp edges, the soft curves,
I ponder this artistry of nature:
how we too form, dissolve, re-form
within the frames of our
own making:
breathe in,
breathe out—the cycle spins:
each flower is a question, a reply,

dancing between the seen
and unseen,
a reminder that all is process,
    that beauty, too,
is a fleeting grace.

Symphony of Currents

the pollen drifts: a golden dance
through shafts of
filtered sunlight,
where air molecules swirl in
silent collusions—
each grain's journey:
a spiral of chance
  and course corrections:
attraction in flux,
repulsion weaving patterns:
a sweet chaos—
the quiet chemistry:
life's whispered pulse,
    unseen currents guiding
their fragile arcs,
each collision a note in
the symphony's rise—

Luminance

dancing in the pond's thin layer:
diatoms spin, light-struck,
photosynthetic whispers
ripple through
each flaring pulse of chlorophyll:
a constant seeking: the sun
baubles in the water,
glinting, alive
what is this flicker of thought?
as life unfurls in
gelatinous forms:
  we ponder:
is awareness merely light?

Lattice of Light

the droplet gathers:
a silver sphere poised,
dancing on the silk strands,
reflecting worlds within worlds—
the web's architecture:
a lattice of intention,
woven in gossamer light,
where tension holds, and flows—
the surface interacts:
cohesion's soft tug,
repulsion's balancing act,
this fragile equilibrium—
each droplet's journey:
a brief but radiant
existence, a moment,
exchanged in the quiet—

Cradle Currents

    in the ocean's warm embrace:
once bright with purpose,
dissolved now
into a cradle for the small
and hungry
and the currents swirl:
a dance of life
stripping the surface:
learners in the
plankton haze,
microbes flourish: entwined
    while sunlight filters,
casting shadows,
    turning waste into homes:
each barnacle
finds refuge,
the cycle flows: sustaining

Twilight Lattice

the streetlamp pulses:
a beacon held
   between dark and light:
the atoms dance
   their probabilistic waltz
in twilight
each photon whispers:
a thread of time,
every flicker carries:
a moment caught,
   in the lattice of evening:
shadows breathe
the ether hums softly:
a wave of change,
where particles shimmer:
in their stillness,
   reminding us:
absence is presence too

Photonics

the sun drips light:
fluid particles
    scatter, bending through
the leaves:
  a dance of photons—where the
eye glances
    each wave an
echo—refracted thoughts
of being: a river's
current, fleeting,
we inhale its shimmer,
suspend it in time
    the quantum leap—a thought,
reality colides with perception: do
    we see the wave?
or catch the glimpse,
as light fluctuates between worlds,
just as we weave our stories,
the threads
of days interlaced in the fabric

Ephemeral Whirl

the ceiling fan spins: a silent
turbulence of air: light sifts
through blades, casting flickers—
shadows dance like thoughts,
in this small room of intention:
each pulse, a moment caught,
the mind skims surface currents:
clouds of dust, suspended, drift—
the flicker pulls me deeper,
into the whirl of transience:
my awareness expands, contracts
like the flicker of a dying star:
what is thought but a brief flick,
a play of tones in light and shade?
each breath syncs with the motion:
the cycle of air, of light:
life coalescing in ways,
like swirls of smoke, each thought
an ephemeral wisp,
winding through the quiet shadows:
in this gentle oscillation,
I find a rhythm bestowed by
the universe's pulse, tides of
perception: continuity wedded
to the ephemeral,
each turn a return.

Catalytic Whispers

enzymes weave in the
cellular twilight:
substrates embrace with such
quiet grace,
   the active sites align:
a gentle kiss,
   unlocking sequences where
thoughts cascade,
  kinship forms in the
fluid substrate's grip:
molecules pulse,
exchanging silent vows,
    each reaction sparking meaning,
perhaps we're all enzymes,
shaped by the dance,
the world hums softly,
its rhythms entwined:
in the depths,
where order meets chaos,
each bond formed, a story,
a binding thread,
   communication flows like
currents unseen,
as the substrate yields to
whispers of change:
  the lattice of life unfurls
its design,
   each choice a reaction,
each moment a spark,
we are but proteins,
folding into the light.

Refraction

   a prism spins the sunlight:
it shatters
  into a cascade of
hues—violet whispers
to the red, a spectrum of longing,
  each color a thought,
each angle a burst
light bends:
a dance of wavelengths,
  the glass a mediator of
unseen truths,
    through transitory moments,
      the knowledge of color's
fleeting embrace

Erosion's Echo

the grains shift:
each little piece a history,
caught in an eddy of wind—
the ocean breathes, it exhales
salty tales of erosion
it whispers to the land,
memory unfurls like the tide:
layer by layer, each grain a
tiny witness to both joy
and loss; the shoreline curves,
its silhouette a soft reminder
of time in constant flow—

Tidal Wisdom

low tide reveals the
barnacle's hold:
a grip on granite:
each crest a home
    to barnacles stacked like
tiny fortresses,
their shells glistening with
a briny sheen,
fragments of the ocean: resilient,
and oh, so fragile,
in their steadfastness.
the wave recedes,
pulling back its dress,
exposing the world beneath
its swells:
anemones sway in the
retreating foam,
while seaweed drapes itself
in emerald,
touching the porous rocks,
soft as breath,
a dance of life suspended in
between the pulls of gravity
and the tide,
a rhythm emerges:
each crash an echo—
the tidal cadence of becoming and
dissolving:
organisms cling and adapt,
    their tenacity a lesson
in persistence,

as change sculpts their
fragile architecture.
time unfurls softly:
the sun's warm glance
works with the ebb and
flow, nurturing
the minuscule thrive and the
vast surround,
    where resilience is woven
through the threads
of existence:
what is held and what is lost—
    the barnacle's wisdom is
the ocean's song.

Mycelial Exchange

beneath the soil: the fungi weave
a lattice of mycelium—thin threads
of whispering connection:
a chatroom
for the roots: exchanging sugars,
    water droplets:
the language of need,
   mapped by enzymes,
signals pulse through
   the dark—a network of giving,
of growth,
each spore a traveler,
bearing gifts—
in this silent exchange:
the forest breathes.

Ephemeral Flux

the night unfurls: a canvas vast as
the cosmos, meteors flicker: bright
strokes of time,
slicing through the
darkness—each a whisper of light, a
crucible of elements: iron, nickel,
  stardust weaving stories in
   and we, beneath this
ephemeral show,
search for warmth within the
cold void,
each moment teeters: a balance
between presence and absence, where
the heart yearns to anchor itself
in the fleeting—yet anchored
  passage, we find solace:
in the arcs
of the sky,
the soft glow of transient
wonders, each trail a reminder:
flux is the language
of being—always.

Pulse of Permeation

beneath the microscope:
a single cell—pulsing,
its membrane—an unbreakable
barrier, yet porous: it
dances with the liquid, absorbing
the ebb and flow of nutrients—
chemical reactions spark, light
up the dark, an electric
echo reverberates: existence,
a cycle of eating and being
and how we, too, entwined in
the web of life, consume air,
the sun's gold kisses our skin:
each breath a momentary,
tender grasp of light reflected
in the droplet's surface
where life clings—small yet vast—
each heartbeat: a rhythm of
the cosmos: nourishment flows
through veins, entwined with time.

Celestial Drift

    the planets wheel in their
silent ballet:
gravity's whisper guiding each arc—
the solar wind carries tales untold
through the void,
where dust settles,
    sculpting the unseen:
a nebula haunts
    the edges of perception,
cradling stars
softly, we drift on the cusp
of orbits:
a single asteroid breaks loose, and
the ripples pulse across
the galactic sea

Stellar Alchemy

a star exists: a blazing forge of
nuclear fusion: hydrogen provides
the sweet alchemy of light and heat
those ancient tales: woven in fire,
   the gods danced in
swirling nebulae:
their fates intertwined
with stellar birth
   as supernovae bloom:
a brilliant death,
   they scatter remnants
like whispers:
   each element a story,
a drumming heart
from dust to dawn and back to dust:
the cosmos speaks in
cycles: infinity,
   the echoes of creation linger

Molecule Dance

the early light: it spills across
the kitchen
counter—fractured patterns,
molecules darting
like hummingbirds,
unavoidable dance of time and dust
a shadow casts:
the knife's edge gleams,
with each slice the
morning expands:
my hands meet the cool steel,
embodying the rhythm of need
behind the window: a world awakens,
  the toast pops up like sprouts
in spring,
yet here: the quiet labor
of breakfast,
a universe contained in
coffee's swirl
as the sun rises:
it proposes change,
the day's unfolding—its
nebulae whisper,
each moment:
both precious and fleeting,
    a continuum laid bare on
this counter.

Twisted Histories

the strands twist:
whorls of history
  not written,
yet felt in each somatic
    pulse that courses through
the living
junk DNA whispers: a language of
silence: a charting of
potential that
dares to ponder identity's breadth
in the nucleus: a cosmos contained—
where proteins dance in
folded finesse
to signify what is,
and what might be
evolution's architecture: ever
in flux: a symphony written in
the quiet,
where each note awaits its play

Spectral Currents

invisible travelers: neutrinos slip
through the fabric of
matter, sighing,
lightweight ghosts of the cosmos,
   weaving stories through the
atom's heart:
what do they know of our density?
they pass unscathed,
like whispers brushed
against the surface of
thought, inhaling
the silence of structures: we built
walls of understanding,
yet here they dance,
unfazed by the weight of existence.
   their presence, a paradox:
we measure
them in the minutiae of time, yet
they escape the nets of certainty,
ghostly hints at the unseen: where
  might they lead,
those sprites of the void?
each collision: a quiet rebellion,
an echo in the vastness
of creation,
an invitation to ponder: how are we
bound, beneath the shadows
of what's felt,
in the transient embrace of
the infinite?
to desire solid answers: a folly,

    as we chase glimmers in
distant realms,
  where knowledge morphs
into spectral forms,
    and uncertainty dons a cloak
  the cosmos breathes:
we are part of its dream.

Stitchery

lichens stitch the granite: silent
interludes of green and gray,
where time's breath etches identity
fungi weave their
threads: mycelium,
intertwined with
algae's light-hungry
tendrils—symbiosis in slow motion
the stone bears witness: centuries
fold into the epidermis of ages,
a testament to the patient earth

Helix

the sunflower turns:
golden spirals trace the sky's
arc, numbers whisper in light—
a sequence blooms, Fibonacci,
each petal a fraction of whole,
nature's algorithm computing—
these curvatures dance:
life unfolds,
as bees hum equations in flight,
the turning earth counts
its breath.

Vital Currents

in the hidden chambers of cells:
where mitochondria pulse with
a rhythm of adenosine triphosphate,
the energy dances, a swirling
cascade: life's own currency—
each organelle a tiny sun:
illuminated in the dark of
cytoplasm—an aqueous embrace,
fluid as thought: they whisper
of symbiosis: the ancient pact—
as glucose flows, a river's
path through membranes, half-hidden
in the folds of existence:
it is a cycle: extraction,
conversion, release—exhale—
we are these rhythms: pulse and
recharge: the vastness of need—
interconnected tendrils: spiraling
in a cosmic web: existence
throbs through every
cell—each beat—

Entangled Currents

the small dance of particles: in
the space between atoms, where
touch is a whisper, a silent echo
rings across quantum fields: when
two become one, the distance folds,
    resonance strikes chords in
like a heartbeat felt from a
hundred miles away:
we drift through
uncertain waves, entangled, caught
in the gravity of shared laughter,
grief's heavy pull: light bends,
    as we reach, stretch,
and bridge the vast—

Hexagonal Symphony

in the hexagonal hush: cells
like dreams stitched in beeswax
with precision: angles echo
the sweet calculus of labor,
each facet an offering, a life.
nectar flows through the prism:
a network woven in air,
the hum of purpose vibrates,
each wing beat a reminder of
what it means to be part and whole.
bodies converge: geometry meets
biology in the dance of light—
a map written in pollen grains,
with stories of sun, rain, and time
that weave together:
the hive sings.
individual arcs, collective lines:
    the waxen architecture
stands ready,
a testament to the unseen hand
that sculpts the symphony of being—
with every hexagon,
new depth emerges.
thus we arrive: in our own forms,
structured yet fluid, we buzz
among the intricate patterns
of soil and sky,
breathing the pulse
    of connection within the
vast weave.

Neon Cartography

under the hum of streetlights:
pigeons wheel between glass towers—
their wings unfurling,
slicing the dusk
as the constellations flicker:
navigational instincts disrupted,
by neon flashes that mimic stars—
each impulse reconfiguring flight:
urban topographies becoming maps,
of adaptation's quiet resilience—

Ebbing Constellations

    sand dollars lie in the
ebbing tide:
a dance of calcium and
shifting shores,
their fragile forms whisper
of ocean's
    infinite breath:
they cradle the sun
    as waves unfurl:
each caress zeros in,
sand grains swirl in a tempest
where life's tenacity:
presses forward,
   while erosion:
gnaws gently at edges
    of memory:
the shoreline unfurls its tale,
as tides pull and push:
an ancient rhythm,
   the rotation of earth:
counteracts stillness,
    even in the silence:
there is motion
the constellation of shells,
we gather now,
reflecting back the cosmos:
found in sand,
the delicate balance:
a fragile knowing,
we are sand dollars:
tracing the brink

Erosion

the tide licks at the edges:
where once was a fortress
of grains,
towering ambitions,
now mere whispers of memory,
  the ocean, relentless,
pulls at the seams:
sunlight refracts through water:
each wave a decay of purpose,
an uninvited sculptor,
remolding the fragile form,
while children laugh,
oblivious to time:

Unfolding

  the proteins unfold:
spirals of life
in aqueous currents: churning and
twisting through uncharted seas of
molecular tides:
each bond a whisper,
echoing back to the primordial brew
  where chaos maps the contours
as amino acids gather:
they find their
places in the grand choreography
of folding: a ballet of hydrophobic
   shifts, charge
interactions: electric,
  a syntax of survival:
every misfolded
gesture a reminder of
transient grace
within the folds, identities bloom:
like neurons connecting in
of thought,
the synapse sparking life
into dreaming patterns:
vast networks
of meaning weaving through the dark
matter of existence:
we are becoming

Porecraft

a kitchen sponge sits:
fibers entwined in
a dance of mitosis:
cells divide, softly
swell: the geometry of
life's simple labor:
water molecules weave:
hydrogen bonds in
delicate symmetry:
every pore a universe:
each droplet holds stories
of the world's pulse:

Ethereal Flux

the water rises: an unseen ballet
where molecules dance,
weaving light through
    the liquid crystal lattice:
bonds break, reform—
  the hum of transition in the
soft warm air
  as heat nudges them:
into the ether, they drift
light as whispers:
a native breath, unspooling
existence: droplets become vapor,
the sky an open palm,
holding stories of change
clouds gather,
a congregation of chaos
    and clarity:
the temperature shifts:
hydrogen atoms—flirt with oxygen,
    spinning in the tension of
the invisible
  each droplet held in
tension—runs dry,
waiting for the moment of
release: the call
of gravity:
we are all caught in cycles,
    the rise, the fall:
we breathe in this void

Prismatic Whispers

the dew drop clings:
fragile and clear
    a prism of light:
scattering its song
    bending realities:
each spectrum a thought
the web dances softly:
in the breath of wind
shifting perceptions:
as colors collide
fragile rainbows whisper:
of fleeting moments

Entangled Grace

   in the soft dusk:
a bee orchid opens
its velvety petals:
a trap of allure
in the air, pheromones swirl:
   the bees dance,
attracted to a shadow
nectar hidden like secrets:
sweet drops
   gleam under the fading light:
bees hover,
guiding their fuzzy bodies:
of need, while separation fades
a cycle of need unspooling:
where one thrives, another obliges,
the orchid's mimicry,
a trick of light:
pollinator and flower entwined,
   the balance precarious:
exists in flux,
each bloom a shimmering
moment: life
   woven with purpose,
each interaction
woven with grace:
a world intertwined

Stardust Whispers

in the quiet expanse of
limitless dark:
nuclear fires
ignite—fusion's dance,
a supernova's brilliance shatters—
light embers scattering through
    from chaos comes the dust
of creation:
new worlds arise,
in their stillness, pulse.
we too emerge—brief flashes
of thought,
each moment a star,
collapsing, brightening,
through birth and decay,
all intersperse,
like stardust swirling,
caught in time's flow,
our whispers dissolve into
cosmic winds,
crafting new narratives from
what was lost.

Thawing Choreography

the ice gives way:
a slow surrender,
fractured patterns of
crystalline light,
beneath: the stirrings of
unseen worlds
bubbles rise:
effervescence of spring,
from the depths:
green tendrils unfurling,
a microcosm awakens: pulses stir
here, where silence once was
a blanket,
life's choreography resumes:
   ebb and flow:
the delicate dance of being

Cosmic Threads

in the quiet pulse of two
distant stars:
photons leap through the fabric
   unseen threads woven tight in
a cosmic loom—
  each flicker,
each twinkling echo of light
a reminder:
what divides us is often
the space that cradles our
shared existence:
  as these particles dance
in synchronicity,
unfurling the mystery
of connection,
   while we sift through the
air between us;
    how the heart mirrors
these entangled paths:
    drawing closer,
yet inching away, unsure:
the universe whispers its
elegant truth.

www.ingramcontent.com/pod-product-compliance
Lightning Source LLC
Chambersburg PA
CBHW060849050426
42453CB00008B/904